KITTEN LADY'S
BIG BOOK OF
Little KITTENS

FOR ELOISE

ALADDIN
An imprint of Simon & Schuster Children's Publishing Division
1230 Avenue of the Americas, New York, New York 10020
First Aladdin hardcover edition October 2019
Text and interior photos copyright © 2019 by Kitten Lady, LLC.
Jacket photo on front cover copyright © 2019 by Kitten Lady, LLC.
Jacket photos on back cover and front flap copyright © 2019 by Andrew Marttila
Interior photos by Hannah Shaw and Andrew Marttila
Interior illustrations by Tiara Iandiorio
All rights reserved, including the right of reproduction in whole or in part in any form.
ALADDIN and related logo are registered trademarks of Simon & Schuster, Inc.
For information about special discounts for bulk purchases, please contact Simon & Schuster Special Sales
at 1-866-506-1949 or business@simonandschuster.com.
The Simon & Schuster Speakers Bureau can bring authors to your live event.
For more information or to book an event contact the Simon & Schuster Speakers Bureau
at 1-866-248-3049 or visit our website at www.simonspeakers.com.
Book designed by Tiara Iandiorio and Karin Paprocki
The illustrations for this book were rendered digitally.
The text of this book was set in Galano Classic Alt.
Manufactured in China 0719 SCP
10 9 8 7 6 5 4 3 2 1
Library of Congress Cataloging-in-Publication Data
Names: Shaw, Hannah René, 1987– author.
Title: Kitten Lady's big book of little kittens / by Hannah Shaw.
Description: New York : Aladdin, 2020. | Includes bibliographical references and index.
Identifiers: LCCN 2019008337 (print) | LCCN 2019009034 (eBook)
ISBN 9781534438958 (eBook) | ISBN 9781534438941 (hardcover)
Subjects: LCSH: Kittens.
Classification: LCC SF447 (eBook) | LCC SF447 .S455 2019 (print)
DDC 636.8/07—dc23
LC record available at https://lccn.loc.gov/2019008337

KITTEN LADY'S
BIG BOOK
OF *Little*
KITTENS

BY HANNAH SHAW

ALADDIN
New York London Toronto
Sydney New Delhi

HI! MY NAME IS HANNAH,

and I'm an **animal advocate** and kitten rescuer. My life is dedicated to protecting the tiniest and most vulnerable **felines**: baby kittens! Over the years, I've saved hundreds of little lives.

I know what you're thinking: "Does that mean you have hundreds of cats?"

NO WAY!

The kittens I rescue are all **foster kittens**.

Fostering is when you give temporary care to a homeless animal. Once the kittens are healthy and old enough, they go to a permanent home with a loving adopter, and then my house is empty so I can save even more kittens.

It's like a revolving door of tiny tigers!

Before

Most of the time, I rescue **orphan kittens** who have been separated from their mothers. Since kittens rely completely on their mothers for warmth, food, and protection, if they are found all alone, they need special help from humans. When kittens don't have a mama, foster parents like me step in and provide the care that they need.

Fostering is the coolest!

ROAR!

I rescue kittens from some of the most unexpected places. I've saved them from underneath houses, on the side of the highway, and even in compost bins and trash cans! Some are only hours old.

Pigeon was found under a dumpster.

Boomba was found in a window well.

The one thing they have in common is that they almost always come from outside, where they are often born to **community cats** who roam freely in the neighborhood.

Teenie Weenie was found in a bush.

Teenie Weenie's mom, Bun, is a community cat!

Without our help, community cats will have lots of kittens, especially during **kitten season**, when the weather is warm and the sun is shining. These kittens can become separated from their moms when well-meaning people pick them up and take them inside.

That's why during the spring and summer, I've always got my hands full! I foster the kittens who end up at my local **animal shelter**, a place that helps lost and homeless animals. When foster parents lend a hand, kitten season is a much happier and safer time for our fuzzy friends!

Tidbit was a newborn kitten found outside all alone at just one day old. When I took him in, he was so small that he fit in the palm of my hand!

Before long, tiny Tidbit blossomed into the cutest little prince.

From this . . .

. . . to this . . .

Now that he's adopted . . . he's the king of the castle.

WHAT AN INCREDIBLE TRANSFORMATION!

But it's not magic—Tidbit just needed lots of hands-on love and care to help him grow.

. . . to this!

Newborn kittens aren't just tiny—they're also totally defenseless. Born with their eyes closed and their ears folded, these little wiggleworms are called **neonatal kittens**, and they need the most help of all.

ANATOMY OF A NEONATAL KITTEN

Tiny cub ears

Closed eyes

Boop-worthy nose

Kissable tummy

Umbilical cord

Nonretractable claws

Jelly bean twinkle toes

These li'l peanuts start to look more like real cats when they open their eyes, from eight to twelve days old. Kittens have blurry vision as babies, but as they get older, they start to be able to see clearly. No matter how their vision is, when kittens open their eyes, I want them to see that the world is a safe place to be a baby cat!

When Mac was first peeking his eyes open, he looked pretty silly, but soon he had big, beautiful baby blues!

Sneak peek!

Tiny kittens can't regulate their own body temperatures, and they need help staying warm when they have no mom to cuddle them. That's why you'll find my kittens snuggling up on a heating pad in a bed of warm blankets! Cozy kittens will start gently **purring** as a sign of comfort.

Sprout loves cuddling with a fluffy stuffed animal. Just don't tell her that her "mom" is actually a dog. . . .

SHHH . . .

Young orphan kittens are **bottle babies**, and they have HUGE appetites. I feed them every few hours, anywhere from six to twelve times a day—even in the middle of the night! When kittens drink from a bottle, their ears will often wiggle with happiness.

Kittens have sensitive tummies and can't digest the milk that many people keep in the refrigerator at home. When a kitten is orphaned, they drink a milk substitute, a special **formula** made just for kittens that has all the nutrients they need to grow into big, strong cats.

YUM!

Boomba loves being pampered!

Believe it or not, kittens and cats are very clean animals. They just need to learn how to **groom** themselves! I brush the kittens with a soft toothbrush, which reminds them of a mother's rough tongue, and it helps them learn how to lick themselves and stay squeaky-clean.

Boomba and Hank love the comforting feeling of getting brushed.

Hank is lookin' fresh!

A full belly and a toothbrush massage can make a kitten sleepy! You've probably heard of a catnap, but have you ever seen a kitten nap? These little snuggle-dumplings are champions of snoozing and will sleep up to twenty-two hours a day. They need lots of rest to support their growth and development.

All that dozing pays off—young kittens gain about one pound every single month.

I place my foster kittens on a small scale to monitor their weight. It's so fun to see them gain weight as they transform from tiny nuggets into mighty minicats. Weighing kittens helps me make sure they're eating right and staying healthy.

GROWTH OF A YOUNG KITTEN

Newborns are light as a feather.

One month, one pound

Two months, two pounds

I also keep kittens healthy by bringing them to a special doctor called a **veterinarian** to get preventative shots and medicine that prepare them for a long and healthy life. The veterinarian's office is usually a kitten's first field trip!

Brave girl at the vet!

If you thought bottle-feeding was messy, just wait until you see a kitten who is **weaning** on to solid food! Kittens become curious about meat around four to five weeks old, so I help them slowly transition from nursing or bottle-feeding to eating on their own. When kittens are first learning how to eat wet kitten food, it's a sloppy adventure. Sometimes more of it gets on their faces than in their mouths.

So yummy!

Margot hasn't quite figured out if food is eaten through your mouth or your foot! After she eats, she sometimes leaves a trail of meaty paw prints behind her. What a mess! She'll figure it out soon. . . .

KITTENS ALWAYS DO!

Do I have something on my face?

⭐ MARGOT ⭐

As kittens begin weaning on to meaty foods, their hunting **instinct** starts to kick in. All felines, like lions, tigers, leopards, and even house cats, are mighty **predators** who have a natural urge to hunt their **prey**. But unlike their wildcat relatives who roam freely on the savanna or in the jungle, house cats are our indoor companions, and their hunting takes the form of playtime.

I spend lots of time playing with my kittens so they can practice their pounce. When these little micropanthers see a toy, they wiggle their butts, leap into the air, and

ATTACK!

Kittens are hilariously awkward while learning how to hunt and play like a cat. When they see a new toy for the first time, they sometimes arch their backs, hop sideways, or poof out their fluffy tails to show how big and intimidating they are.

It's so entertaining to see them make funny movements when they are surprised!

Kittens also have instincts to climb, perch, and hide. While their wildcat relatives can be found lounging in trees and hiding in tall grasses, our feline companions only have the environment that we create for them in our homes. These kitties need lots of environmental **enrichment** to help them stay happy and healthy in an indoor setting by allowing them to express their natural instincts.

Look at Pigeon climb!

Small Fry loves tunnels!

Finn's favorite
place is the very top
of the cat tree, where
he can look down and
oversee everything from a
bird's-eye view.

Of course, the best way to keep kittens happy is for them to have a friend. Just like you and me, kittens love having a buddy to play with. Having a companion helps them feel confident and endlessly entertained. There's nothing quite as special as feline friendship!

Fritter and Jelly have been best friends since the day they were born! They are a **bonded pair**, which means they'll always stay together, even when they're adopted.

Friends fur-ever

Thanks for saving us!

Once they are healthy and at least eight weeks old, the kittens are ready to say hello to their future family and **forever home**, where they'll stay for their whole lives.

People who are looking for a new companion or two can apply to adopt kittens just like mine through their local animal shelter or rescue group. If they are a good fit and are ready for the responsibility of caring for a pet, they can meet the kittens and bring them home. It's so exciting to help kittens find their perfect match!

When it's time to say goodbye to my foster kittens, I have a lot of different emotions. I might feel a little sad to part ways, but I mostly feel very proud of them for graduating from foster care. **Adoption** day is a celebration!

Fostering helps kittens go from tiny and helpless to big and strong. By dedicating a few weeks of time to helping them grow, anyone can make a big difference for little kittens!

After the kittens get adopted, I feel so happy knowing that I saved their lives.

AND MY HOME ISN'T EMPTY FOR LONG . . .

BECAUSE
THERE ARE
ALWAYS

#1

We ♥ CUDDLES!

CHEESE!

MORE KITTENS
WAITING TO BE
SAVED!

GLOSSARY

Adoption: the act of giving a permanent home to an animal

Animal advocate: a person who supports the welfare of animals

Animal shelter: a facility designed to help lost, abandoned, and homeless animals find a home

Bonded pair: two cats who are close friends and are adopted together

Bottle babies: young kittens who drink from a bottle

Community cats: unowned, free-roaming cats who live outdoors in the community

Enrichment: an enjoyable activity that helps an animal express his or her natural behaviors

Felines: members of the cat family

Forever home: a home where an animal lives with a family for the duration of his or her life

Formula: a milk substitute with special ingredients just for kittens

Foster kittens: kittens who are living in temporary homes in preparation for adoption

Fostering: providing a temporary home to an animal, with the goal of finding him or her a permanent home

Groom: when a cat cleans himself or herself by licking

Instinct: a natural urge to express a behavior

Kitten Season: the warm season when lots of kittens are born and need help from foster families

Neonatal kittens: tiny newborn kittens

Orphan kittens: kittens who have become separated from their mothers and need special care

Predators: animals who hunt

Prey: animals who are hunted

Purring: making a gentle, rumbling sound of contentment

Veterinarian: a special doctor for cats, dogs, and other animals

Weaning: the transition from nursing or bottle-feeding to eating independently

FIVE WAYS KIDS CAN BE SUPERHEROES FOR CATS

1. Get Crafty! There are so many helpful items you can make for your local animal shelter, like DIY fleece blankets, cat beds, community cat shelters, and awesome cat toys! You can even make some fun adoption posters for the kitties that need help finding a home and hang them up around your community.

2. Fundraise! Whether you host a lemonade stand, a bake sale, or even a gallery of your best cat drawings, there are lots of creative ways to raise a few bucks for our feline friends. Every dollar helps, and you'll feel so proud bringing your donation to your local organization!

3. Collect Food! These hungry kitties need a ton of food, so why not help your local shelter by doing a cat food drive at your school or community center? Ask your friends, family members, and teachers to chip in with some cans of wet food or bags of kibble.

4. Volunteer! Sometimes animal organizations will have kids help with cleanup, assist with special tasks, or even quietly read to cats who need a little bit of comfort and company. What better way to practice your reading skills than with a furry friend? Ask your local rescue group how kids can lend a hand.

5. Be an Advocate! Educate your friends and classmates about cats and kittens! Next time you get to choose a topic for a school project, consider sharing what you know about cat and kitten rescue. Spread the word and encourage everyone to be compassionate to cats!

AUTHOR'S NOTE

Thank you for inspiring kids to be kind! Children are naturally compassionate and curious about animals, and I hope that this book opens their eyes to the wonderful world of kitten advocacy.

If you're interested in saving little kittens too, don't be afraid to look into fostering. It's a fantastic summer activity for families! During the warm months when children are out of school, kitten season is in full effect—and shelters need lots of help. Fostering can help teach kids responsibility from a young age and can make a huge difference for the animals in your community!

There are many feline populations that need the love of a foster family. If you're not ready for the responsibility of caring for young orphans, I recommend talking to your local shelter about fostering more independent weaned kittens, or providing a foster home for nursing moms with babies! Caring for a mama cat and her kittens can be a great way for kids to experience the joy of rescue, and to save little lives (with a little maternal assistance). Kids can lend a hand by playing and socializing with the kittens, cleaning, and even providing some special care with supervision from an adult. Kids and grown-ups make a great cat-saving team.

Another important way you can protect kittens is to spay and neuter your pet cats and the community cats in your neighborhood! With hundreds of thousands of kittens entering shelters every year in need of assistance, one of the most responsible things advocates can do is to participate in spay and neuter programs. Let's work together to make the world a safer place for cats and kittens!

Ready to start? Get all the information you need about finding a foster program, how to set up your home base, how to provide care to kittens, and more at KittenLady.org.